Prayers for Comfort in Difficult Times

for Joan and Nancy

fondly

Zuita

Prayers for Comfort in Difficult Times

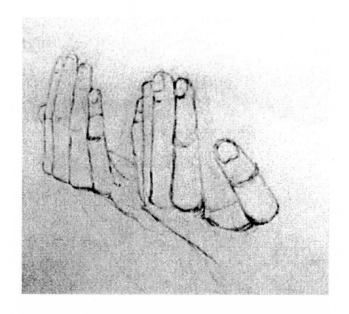

Marguerite Guzmán Bouvard, Ph.D.

First edition

International Standard Book Number 1893239330
Library of Congress Control Number 2004111699

Acknowledgments

The author wishes to thank the editors of the magazines in which the following prayers appeared:

"Giving Thanks For Your Lessons" — *Healing Ministry Magazine, Fall 2002.*

"We Are One" — *Healing Ministry Magazine, Summer 2003.*

"Learning to See" — *National Catholic Reporter the Independent Weekly, February 15, 2002.*

"What Silence is For" — *National Catholic Reporter the Independent Weekly, December 12, 2003.*

"Praising the Journey" — *Santa Fe Broadside* (http://sfpoetry.org/October2002.html)

"Questions" — *Bearing Witness 2: The Best of the Observer Arts Magazine*, edited by Wayne Brown, *the Jamaica Observer, 2001*

"Honoring the Hidden Work," "Mindfulness," and "Questions" were set to music by the Boston composer Ruth Lomon and performed by the Boston Secession, a professional vocal art ensemble directed by Jane Ring Frank on March 26, 2004. They will appear in a forthcoming CD of Ruth Lomon's work.

Drawings by Deborah R. Huacuja.

Front Cover — window by Georges Roault in church of Notre-Dame de Toutes Graces.

For Brad Saul

Table of Contents

Foreword

When the Canon Devemy founded the church of Notre-Dame de Toutes Graces in the Plateau d'Assy in the French Alps for the patients in the tubercular sanatorium in the 1950s, he shocked the Church establishment by calling upon modern artists of all faiths and political leanings to lend their talents. He made the call because, in his own words, "Every true artist is inspired, is already prepared for, predisposed to spiritual insight: why, then, would he not be predisposed to the coming of the Spirit itself which, after all, blows where it will." He also asked the patients to paint a mural for the crypt, a work of such glowing colors that most visitors would conclude it was completed by a prominent artist.

As a poet, a scholar, and above all a woman who has been struggling with two debilitating chronic illnesses for many years, I too have found myself inspired to give voice to the fruits of my visions and inner growth. These prayers are a witness to the spiritual journey of living with pain and the illumination that comes from suffering. In our society, we view illness and any misfortune as problems to be solved, ignoring the emotional toll of physical pain as well as the spiritual awakening that often accompanies prolonged distress. I had always felt a profound faith, but the transformation of my daily life helped me to renew and deepen it rather than to reject it, although even the strongest beliefs are often buffeted by events. That renewal was also sparked by solitude as I could no longer pursue a busy schedule or spend much time in social situations. I discovered that my solitude gave me much room for reflection, nourishing my soul and giving me the courage to find a path for myself where there apparently was none. I learned not just to survive, but also to live fully, richly and to be of use to people who were experiencing a myriad of losses. Becoming available to one's core on an ongoing basis is to discover the commonality of our pain, joy, confusion, and wonder.

Illness, loss, and living in troubled times can be viewed as opportunities. Even though I was faced with so many constraints on my time and energy, I came to see my situation as not only demanding a renegotiation of my days, but as a moral occasion. Because of my physical limitations and the brush with mortality that all serious illness entails, I found myself reassessing how I would spend my time, for now I had none to squander. I knew that who I would become and what I would do would have to be spiritually meaningful. Thus, the work of deep reflection became a way of life and a path to connect with the world in new ways. Given the difficult period we live in and my life-long concern with social justice, reflection became a way of both filtering out the static of violence and aggression and of focusing on the good and quiet people in this world. Reflection also gave me an opportunity to experience the world in a new way, to appreciate the beauty and mystery of the creation as well as the blessings in my life, almost as if I had been granted a second sight. I found myself open to the world in new ways, to experiences I would pass by if I were rushing from one task to another as I had done in my former life. Just as cosmologists are discovering new dimensions in our universe, there are more levels of personal awareness than we may realize. What I learned and what is mirrored in these prayers is the wonder at our doorstep, the joy of kind gestures, and a wider perspective on harrowing occurrences at home and abroad.

Thus, this book of prayers is about the human condition with all its hopes, disappointments, losses, passions and joys. It is intended to be a companion one can turn that reflects our journey, supporting us through difficulties while giving us a vision that enriches our life. One of these in a profound compassion for all of humanity and also for our own weakness and what we perceive as failures, a quality that helps us transcend our problems as well as opening us to a much wider world.

Living with this illness hour by hour, confronting it head on awakened me to a world that is so immense. I discovered that the spirituality I thought I had was very different from this learning through patience and endurance, that I deepened my understanding of life now that I had so much time to reflect and that this slow awakening is part of what we called soul.

An important part of my coping became my practice of daily spiritual meditation. It helped me to confront my own pain and face head on whatever I was feeling. My hour of sitting every evening before preparing dinner, of going into meditation in the most unlikely places such as the waiting room of a physician's office, gave me new insights. I began reviewing each day not in a negative or punitive way, but naming the richness, the play of light on the pine tree outside my window, a visit with a friend, the personal growth of my adult children. I became more aware of each moment, grateful for the possibilities and the sacredness of the ordinary, practicing mindfulness, as the Buddhists would call it. I found that I thus acquired a sense of spaciousness in a life I once found constricted by physical problems.

These prayers I formed spontaneously during my meditations are not only concerned with the work of loss but also with living well in the difficult circumstances we must all traverse. Illness or any kind of grief does not define a person; it is a strand in the rich if often fraught tapestry of daily life. Coping with our frailties does not exempt us from the problems we all face. Nor does it exclude the times of affirmation and praise for the endless marvels of the creation, shattering the myth that people who live with trying circumstances do not experience fullness or contentment.

Anyone who is ill or dying, or who suffers from a particular loss experiences many assaults on his or her self-esteem: This is an issue I struggle with continually. The prayers in the first section seek to validate and respond to these feelings, addressing the sense of loneliness and isolation that are part of this journey. In one of them, I recall the many people who have been an important part of my life over the years even though they have died. Like so many of us, I am often blinded by sorrow, unable to see my tether of light, the presence of God's love in my soul.

Anger is an integral part of living with difficult situations and I honor it in one of the prayers. Once I began my meditation with the plea to help me move beyond anger, and when I stopped short, thinking, "No, I need to be here, to feel this." I learned that an anger that is not directed at others, but is a just outrage at a situation has its own authenticity and dignity.

As the years passed, I found myself radically changing my values, asking for wisdom and understanding rather than for measuring up to social standards of success, recognizing the enormity of kind gestures and especially feeling how deeply I am connected to every living thing. Persistent prayer and meditation have taught me much about life, have given me an insight into its depth: that the world is not just noise and destruction, but is also held together by the goodness of both the holy and the ordinary who walk among us, giving of themselves so that we may all prosper; that sorrow is part of the completion of our lives and enables us to experience moments of intense joy. I learned that although our lives seem so fleeting, they are suffused with the qualities of eternity. The sections entitled "Affirmation" and "Thoughts" celebrate the new awareness I gained during this journey.

The final section "Praise" is an expression of the joy and thankfulness for the succor, awareness and blessings we continue to experience regardless of our situations.

There is much healing in the silence of one's own heart. We learn to be present to ourselves, listen carefully to others, accept the unexplainable and feel a deep reverence for the gift of life.

Illness

Seeing You At My Side

Divine Creator,

when I feel alone

on my difficult journey

through illness

may I see each person

who accompanies me

with understanding and compassion

as expressions of Your love.

Prayer For Courage

When I face an icy rock-strewn

river that separates morning

from evening, may I not hold

back. Divine Creator,

help me to move beyond

the seeming safety

of denial, to ford the river

of my emotions

with each muscle in my heart.

Help me to honor

this passage, to appreciate

that moments of just anger

have their own dignity,

their own fierce beauty.

Feeling Lost

Sometimes my illness is a room

without windows or doors,

a prison no one can see.

I smile at people around me

as the day unfolds,

but I walk at the margins

of the world,

not in it. Dear God

reach out your hand,

lead me home.

Prayer For Self-Esteem

May I remember

that I am more than

overwhelming fatigue

that I am passion

and have possibilities.

May I see clearly

through the film

of sorrow, through the film

of despair.

May I awaken

to Your loving presence

and always remember

I am Your child.

The Grace of Receiving

Help me to cut through the thickets

of pride when I am overwhelmed

by need. May I become open.

May I lean towards

the way branches reach out

for passing swaths of light,

for a breeze laying its hands

on outstretched arms,

for soothing words.

Overcoming Discouragement

Divine Healer,

You have helped me

in so many ways.

Humbly I ask

that I may be healed

of discouragement.

Grant me the strength

to begin again,

to live my life

as if it were new.

The Insights of Suffering

May I cherish each day,

however empty or futile

it may seem —

may I honor the invisible

work of pain and sorrow,

knowing that it will find

a voice, and remembering

that such times

are part of completion.

Overcoming Fear

Teach me how to float free

from my body's terror,

my heart's anxiety.

Help me to learn the wisdom

of leaves buoyed

by the invisible,

to trust that the seemingly invincible

weight I bear will yield

the way night surrenders to dawn.

Learning To See

Grant me the vision

to see leaves on naked

branches, to hear birdsong

in the stillness of winter,

to sense water flowing

beneath its skin of ice.

Letting Go

Teach me to let go

with grace

when my legs

no longer carry me

and my strength falters.

Help me transform the grief

over my body's frailties

into the peace

of surrender.

The Work Of Faith

Divine Creator, help me

to understand with my whole

being that the end

of a life is also

the beginning of a vaster

life that we who are left behind

cannot imagine

and that even though

we must loosen all bonds

when we ourselves depart

the love we experience

in this brief existence

will endure.

Difficult Times

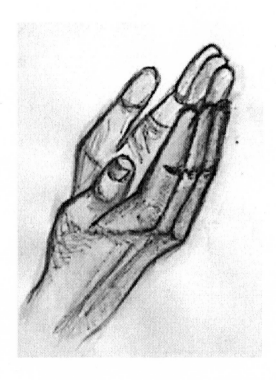

Anger

When in the midst of dailiness

those around me

wound me with their actions

and words, may I not drown

in anger. Dear God help me to free

myself of this burden

that weighs me down

and only deepens the pain,

blinding me to the good moments,

obscuring Your presence.

Grief

Dear God, the death

of my loved one

has left me broken

and rudderless with empty days

stretching before me.

Lead me out of silence

towards a new path,

heal the anguish

in my heart,

make me whole again.

Learning Perspective

I know a vast invisible world

throbs beside our own.

It has called to me

during moments of calm.

Divine Creator,

let me not be trapped

in the problems of dailiness,

in irritation and grief.

Help me to open the eyes

of my inner self

until there are no veils

between worlds.

Holding On To What Matters

When the values around me

seems distorted

help me to remember

that our true measure

is not external.

Help me to remember

that what we call success

fades, that acts of kindness

are the markers

of our days.

Divine Creator,

help me to realize

that although they may

seem invisible,

such gestures are written

in eternal ink.

Asking For Guidance

May I walk in wisdom

and understanding, the wisdom

to find a path where

there is none, the understanding

to accept the people I meet,

so that I may hear

with their ears,

feel their hidden

tempests, see them

in relation to themselves

rather than to me.

Hidden Loss

Dear God, help me

to bear the weight

of a loss so invisible

to others, of coming close

to a cherished dream

only to have it

slip away beyond

my reach. Help me

to rediscover hope.

Forgiveness

May I learn to forgive

those who have caused me

harm, who have hurt me

knowingly or unawares

as You forgive us

our thoughtless and selfish

acts. May I realize

how futile it is

to dwell on the past,

how freeing to take

each day as a new

page, to see the humanity

in each person

who has caused us grief.

Prayer For Strength Of Heart

When war rages like marauding winds

tearing us apart and fear

stalks the land pitting neighbor

against neighbor, may I not be shaken

like a leaf but hold fast

to my own thoughts.

When rampant cruelty begets

indifference may I not turn

away but let myself be scalded

by another's pain.

Seeing The Good All Around Us

Let me not be overwhelmed

by the tumult, noise

and destruction that surround

me. May I take refuge

in that vast, invisible

world where the footprints

of long gone saints

give off light

and the saints who walk

among us with ordinary

faces quietly doing Your work

hold it all together.

Mindfulness

May I not be caught

in the turbulence of my days,

but awaken to the moon glowing

through branches, tufts

of new grass among

melting snow.

May I always remain

a child, drawn

by wonder at what is.

Lesson

Merciful God, help me to grasp

this most difficult lesson —

that learning to honor

and love myself

during life's daily battles

is a way of honoring You.

Endurance

May I see my trials

as opportunities for learning

to think in new ways.

May I walk through them

with dignity and grace.

May I learn to find

the light in darkness.

Seeking Reassurance

Divine Creator,

in times of uncertainty

help me to remember

that you are

our only certainty.

When the world trembles

with so much suffering

and destruction,

when I cannot fathom

the endless horror and grief,

awaken me to the pure

simplicity of trust

in your Divine plan.

Trusting The Invisible World

Sometimes with a flash

of knowing, You let me see

that what lies before us

is so much smaller than

it appears, that a deeper meaning

rises unseen before us.

When I sorrow for this battered

and troubled world,

or for my own suffering, help me

towards that knowing,

that vastness my mind

cannot fathom.

Affirmations

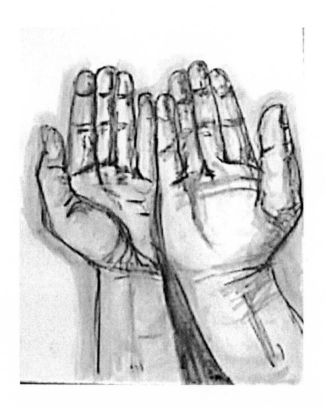

I Am Accompanied

The times I felt as if

I were abandoned

in a field of bare rocks

You reminded me

that I carry every person

who has loved me,

each life who has touched mine,

that I hold within me

many different voices,

many cherished faces

I can turn to again and again.

I Am Part Of You

Divine Creator

When I struggled

to think well of myself,

You spoke to me

in my heart,

"No one who loves Me

is worthless."

Reprieve

The way the first light

seeps through drawn curtains,

You draw me out of loneliness

with the memory

of unexpected kindness

from friends who gave

so freely and with such

joy. The way light reappears

in slow increments

revealing the solidity

of my desk and books,

You trace the outline

of a road back

from the exile of despair.

At The Threshold

Divine Creator

as I cried out

"How can I walk through

my bone-deep fear

not of death, but of dying?"

You answered

"Think of it as part

of the work of living,

taking one step

at a time, one breath

and then another."

Renewal

After months of raw pain and no sleep,

when each day rises above me

like a precipitous mountain,

suddenly my spirit returns

like new grass, spreading

its cloak on the bruised earth,

speaking the language

of winds. Again and again

You bring me back

to the simplicity and grace

of the soul's new shoots.

What Holds Us

Even when the world

seems upside

down, when hatred

and violence race across

the land like a fire

raging out of control,

You remind me there is a light

that is never extinguished.

You remind me

that even in the worst

of times when we face

each other with words

unsheathed like knives

there is a wisdom

that embraces us all.

Prayer For Growth

Divine Creator, when I cried out

to You because I couldn't change

my way of thinking,

You answered,

the power lies deep

within you, and I felt

the mountains inside

give way.

Choice

Divine Creator, You have given us

the precious gift of free will.

With every breath and even in the worst

of circumstances we can choose

to find meaning. We can seek out beauty

in the most unlikely places, be truthful

when faced with deception,

open ourselves up to learn

new ways of living fully.

May we use this freedom

to discover Your Holy will,

serving it in peace and joy.

Prayer For A Wounded Marriage

Dear God, bless this man and this woman.

May they find a path through

their anger and their grief,

the brambles of misunderstanding.

They still yearn for the time

when they stood before You, their love

for each other a bouquet fragrant

with wonder and joy.

Help them to grow, to learn patience,

to see at this late hour

how they are each other's sustenance.

Guide them on this journey,

show them the road back.

Aging

As I age and my body's disabilities

multiply, narrowing the space

in which I live, I reflect

on Your many blessings:

the richness of my accumulated

experience and my increasing ability

to share it with those in need.

As time wears down

my physical self, I experience

a growing awareness of my soul.

Dear God, I see You

everywhere, I feel Your nearness.

Hope

When I was feeling broken

by the ravages of illness, by its litany

of humiliations and invisible

losses, suddenly

there came a flickering

inside me of what can never

be destroyed, Your light,

Your beloved presence,

bringing me back

from the abyss.

We Are One

I come before you

as part of every living thing;

the clump of violets

at the edge of a fence

after the first frost,

the child carrying a whole

country's famine in his scream,

the man sleeping

on the street with only

a carton for shelter.

May I walk in Your grace.

May I walk in your blessings.

May I rejoice in Your

love where there is neither

great nor small.

Creator All Wise

Divine Creator,

You accompany me

not by granting my wishes,

but with gifts that I didn't have

the wisdom to ask for

and that sustain me

in ways I could never

have imagined.

Joy

When I am deep in prayer

I am sometimes flooded

with a joy that sweeps

my whole being.

Divine Creator

could this be a taste

of life after death,

an awakening of such

proportions the body/self

is too small to encompass it?

Thoughts

The Holy Book

It is the doorway

into our beginnings,

the cloud of feathery

green shoots rising

from that cosmic tree.

Humility is written there

and grandeur.

Our seeing deeply

into all that surrounds us,

our awakening, all inscribed

in the body's sacred text.

Power

When the headlines seem to clang

like destiny and unexploded bombs

transform watermelon fields

into thieves of sons, I turn

to the ocean thundering

Your pronouncements,

the green lights, the dizzying plumes

in its upturned waves

scattering Your radiance.

I study the grass, its spiky

shoots rising from the sand —

life ever burgeoning

despite us.

Reaching Out

The world around me

with its seemingly invincible

problems, with its armies,

and its cruel laws tries to tell

me that I can do nothing

against it. But You have taught me

how a quiet word, an outstretched

hand to those who are in pain,

has divinity and how giving

of oneself is the breath

of life that can never

be quenched, a tiny spark

that reflects Your light.

Your Splendor

In late afternoon I strolled

By the lake with my loved one,

the light thick and honeyed,

the lake burning

like smoked glass. I could only walk

at a snail's pace

and with great pain. But my hand

in his was a bird,

and the shore etched itself

on my whole body: water

glowing through a lattice

of shrubs, grandfather trees,

the earth underfoot

yielding and sustaining.

Dear God of everlasting

love, I know that his hand

enfolding mine

and the splendor around me

was Your reflection.

Beyond Destruction

Always in history's scrolls,

fists are razing

temples, torching

holy books, silencing

gongs and bells.

But always we are redeemed

by children, by the hunger

in every new person

for what we cannot see,

for the spirit that beckons.

Journey Through Night

Nights I count my fears

as if I were fingering beads;

the body's slow betrayal, the upturned

palm left empty, and the darkness

without a seeming exit

when a voice moves through me

telling me that doubt

is only one of my hands

clasping the other called faith.

What Silence Is For

To hear the flames' brisk whoosh

between logs,

the crackle of my thoughts.

To watch clouds blurring trees,

houses, slopes, swallowing the mountain,

wrapping me in their soft breathing.

To let go of boundaries, become

grass, leaf, rain.

To reach a knowing beyond

my flesh and bones.

Listening To The Trees

Now more than ever I turn

to the quiet world of trees.

Their presence stirs me awake

as if I were seeing for the very first time

the pin oak's massive trunk, its totemic scars,

the sugar maple's frothing ocean,

and lindens embracing the air.

I cry out — oh, pin oak, sugar maple, beech

and linden with your mysterious

horizons, oh my mother, my grandmother,

my vanished friends. Those sheltering trees,

rectors of earth and of the meridians

of heaven are whispering: *Open the pages*

of our ancient texts. What you love

 is all around you.

Questions

I ask why this stone

in my breast.

You answer with a waterfall

kneading rocks through its fingers.

When a flash flood of tears

sweeps over my borders

and I shake my fist at the empty air,

You remind me how music is born.

When I question the history books,

the phalanxes of raw recruits

torn from their mothers' arms,

You answer I am a minnow

trying to chart the ocean.

When I fill my quiver with arrows,

more questions ripping the blue air,

You tell me to ponder the text

of the buttercups

in the field outside my window.

Forms Of Prayer

1

A longing that issues
from a cello,
annihilating time.

2

Befriending a stranger,
speaking with
an enemy.

3

Bearing the weight
of our hardships
with quiet grace.

4

Planting olive trees
in the chambers
of the heart.
Tilling fields
for the next generation.

Our Passage

Evenings, the mountain returns

to itself with the sleepy twittering of birds,

the immensity of slopes – returns

to its own order where we are guests

skirting the edges, barely beginning

to plumb its mysteries.

Evenings recall the blessings

of completion, feeling

closer to the mysteries

of our brief passage,

its dreamlike unfurling,

its moments deeply lived

touching eternity.

Praise

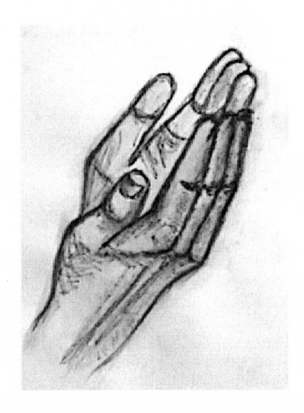

Your Life-Giving Presence

You are my food and drink,

the breath that swaths

my heart, binding us

together. You are the nourishment

of my soul, the music

in my blood, the voice

that never dies.

Seeing Beneath Our Differences

Praising You, I praise

Your name in the languages

of all faiths, every ceremony

that celebrates Your presence,

each face that turns towards

Your light with anguish

and with hope.

The Blessing Of Rice And Water

When the tea- kettle hums on the stove

may I remember the women

standing on line for water

from Kosovo to Fallujah,

and when I am cooking

for my family may I remember

the distended bellies

of the children in Haiti

and hear their high sweet

voices in my room.

May I honor the blessings

of rice, thyme and clear water,

and always remember

the whole world is one body.

Lighting Candles

Nights, while lying awake,

I light candles for the people

I love asking for their healing

as if I were in silent naves

where centuries whisper

their secrets. I light one taper

after another as haloes

of air vibrate above each flame

like new breath. It is a way

of giving You thanks

for their presence in my life,

a way of loving You.

.

Honoring The Hidden Work

Praise the spider's work

of weaving, the monarch butterflies

criss-crossing the frigid air

over continents and the rock worm

laying foundations for cathedrals

of coral reefs. Praise the loom

that is never stilled

the persistence

and strength of fragility.

Praise The Wounded

Praise the child

in the wheelchair

for he is whole.

Praise the blind man

for he sees

in a different way.

Praise the deaf woman

who hears

with all of her body

and the person who is deaf

and blind for she can feel

the air vibrate long

after the swans have flown.

Praise The Hand

Praise the hand that guides needle

and thread, that ushers

clay into eloquence.

Praise the hand that patiently

repairs what is broken,

the hand that coaxes music

out of metal scrap.

Praise the hand in the hand

that moves beyond

the brevity of flesh.

Praising The Beauty Of The Creation

Praise the sky releasing its waters

of light and the trees singing

in the stillness. Praise the ancient language

of roots and the plum bush

dreaming its smoky blues.

Praise the field spinning

its web of wild shallots

and the grass washing the air

with its flames.

Honor the day tumbling on

like a river in so many

accents and colors.

Praising The Journey

May I make of my life a prayer,

wearing my years like a tree;

its flocks of leaves singing

their tender vibratos,

its gaunt limbs pouring

blue rivers of shadow

over snow. May I honor

the wounds inscribed

on my body. During times

of drought may I plumb

the holy water of rain

in my heart.

Giving Thanks For Your Lessons

Help me to remember

that because of You,

I am not naked before

blows, but clothed

with gifts that grow

over time. Thank You for teaching me

patience, for the flexibility

of the willow, for courage

to scale the mountains

within myself. Thank You

for the vision to hold moments

of delight as if they were

carved of jade. Thank You

for the beauty of lichen

blooming on an aged tree,

for teaching me that grief

and joy are married

like sap and earth.

.

About The Author

Marguerite Guzmán Bouvard is the author of four books and two chapbooks of poetry including the prize-winning *Journeys Over Water*. She has also written a number of books on human rights and *The Path Through Grief, A Compassionate Guide*. She is on the editorial advisory board of the *Healing Ministry Magazine*, for caregivers of the ill and dying. She was a professor for many years and is currently a Scholar with the Women's Studies Research Center at Brandeis University.

About The Artist

Deborah R. Huacuja was born in Monterrey, Neuvo Leon, Mexico, and grew up in Mexico City. She studied fine arts at the Bezalel Academy in Jerusalem, the Avni Institute in Tel Aviv and the Mason Gross School of the Arts at Rutgers University. Her work has been widely exhibited and is in a number of private collections. She has been a featured artist of the First Night Celebration of the Arts in Boston and her piece "Libertad" is the inspiration for the 2005 event's promotional materials.

Printed in the United States
22623LVS00005B/352-369